LOVE JESUS!

LESSONS IN PASSING

SUSAN RODEBAUGH HADDEN

COLLECTED BY BILL RODEBAUGH

ISBN 978-1-64300-876-9 (Paperback)
ISBN 978-1-64300-877-6 (Digital)

Covenant Books, Inc.
11661 Hwy 707
Murrells Inlet, SC 29576
www.covenantbooks.com

Introduction

"$\mathcal{L}$ove Jesus" was the final entry in our daughter Susan's Journal, written on Jan. 25, 2018. The last because shortly after the entry Susan could not concentrate or physically write or type.

"Lessons In Passing" exhibits a love of Christ, family and friends. They come from the heart of a young mother who was saved through the blood and sacrifice of our Lord and Savior, Jesus Christ.

Her name is Susan Edith (Rodebaugh) Hadden. Susan changed her home address from Pennsburg, PA to Heaven on March 29, 2018. She died at the age of 42 from myo-epithelial carcinoma.

Susan was a wife and mother of four; husband of 19 years Bob and children; Bobby, Matthew, Emily and Nathan.

Born Jan. 28, 1967, Susan tipped the scales at 10lbs and 10ozs to Bill and Eydie Rodeabugh with an older brother, Bill Jr. She was truly a beautiful and miraculous little baby. She slept through the night from the second day she came home from the hospital.

Susan grew into a loving, strong willed and highly principled daughter and sister. The hallmark of her life was her love of Christ.

She attended Cedar Grove Christian Academy in Phila. And was graduated from Phila. College of Bible with degrees in Bible and Elementary Education. She became a Christian School elementary teacher, wife, mother and hardworking church administrative assistant.

In June 2017, Susan fell and broke her hip. The repair wasn't completely successful, and she spent months in severe pain. Pain so intense that it caused her tears and a desire to "go Home".

Her pain wasn't generated completely by the hip injury. It was discovered to also be the result of brain tumors and other inoperable tumors. She was diagnosed with cancer on Oct. 21, which was her mom and dad's 50th anniversary.

Susan spent from early Nov. 2017 until March 29, 2018 in a bed in her dining room/office watching the earth get cold and barren. Snow falling reminding you of the Christmas Carole – "In the Bleak Midwinter".

We believe that Susan knew it was only a matter of time before she would be home with the Lord but sorry that she would not be here for her family.

With her last words – Love Jesus- Susan not only asks believers to live up to their commitment they made when they accepted Christ as their savior but to those who may read her words and come to Christ.

So, after you read Susan's "Lessons in Passing" ask yourself this, "Where am I in my relationship to Christ?" If you do not have a personal relationship with Him read the Bible beginning with the Gospel of John. John's Gospel is filled with promises. The best promise is found in chapter 3 and verse 16: "For God so loved the world that He gave

His only Son, that whoever believes in Him shall not perish but have everlasting life."

You can accept Christ simply by recognizing Him as Lord and savior of your life. God knows your heart. It's not complicated and you don't eloquent words. A simple prayer (conversation) will do. Something like this will do, "Lord Jesus, I want to thank you for dying for me on the cross. I want to open the door of my life and receive you as my savior and Lord. Thank you for taking away my sins and giving me the promise of eternal life. Help me to be the person you want me to be."

So the message of our daughter Susan's life is simple, just LOVE JESUS and everything else will fall into place because God has a plan for our life.

November 14 at 10:44 a.m.

*H*i friends! I am home and so blessed to have the opportunity to be home and getting stronger every day.

We are praying that God be glorified through this . . . We know He is going to continue to do the amazing!

We are so thankful for your prayers and would ask that they could continue!

I will post here as much as possible . . . to keep everyone up to date. 😊

November 17 at 9:07 a.m.

Hi, friends.

*J*ust wanted to thank all of you for your prayers and just everything. I am doing well . . . getting more strength every day. I am excited to see the sun/sky every morning! God gives me another day to enjoy Him and His creation.

Thank you so much for the prayers . . . we are praying with anticipation that God is going to do something amazing.

If I haven't said thank you personally I am doing it now.

I'm sitting up in my chair right now enjoying the sun. God is GREAT!

November 20 at 7:08 a.m.

*M*onday morning, my friends! See this week as how you can serve Jesus through serving others! It's a short week, so totally doable!

I am feeling great . . . the nights sometimes are long and hard . . . but praying through is how I make it.

Keep praying that Jesus be glorified through all of this! I would love to see you! Text me! I love you all and am praying for you! 😊

November 21 at 6:29 a.m.

Tuesday before Thanksgiving

*T*hank someone today for something . . . something you may have never thanked them for before! Encourage someone today!

I know it's a busy week, especially because you are gearing up for the big meal . . . and I have the great blessing of sitting back and it being done for me . . . so I thought I would focus on saying thank you to all of you. Every day I am flooded with cards . . . and I want to say thank you so much . . . I read everything, and I am so blessed by your words and prayers. These are the beautiful flowers I received yesterday from Alissa Dell'Olio Messina . . . thank you so much . . . they are a blessing to wake up to this morning since it's still dark out.

Have a wonderful Tuesday!

November 22 at 8:25 a.m.

*W*ednesday awesome! This man is amazing . . . he vacuums my hair off everything . . . everyday . . . never complains. He gets me dressed . . . loves me . . . etc. I don't have enough time to list all of his chores that he does just because he loves me. He is my greatest blessing, and I am so sad that I didn't realize it earlier!

Wives . . . look for GOOD in your hubby! Of course, there are things that you would change, but God made him that way!

November 24 at 7:14 a.m.

Black Friday~

I only went Black Friday shopping one time that I can remember. The hustle and bustle was exciting . . . I guess. My daughter went this year with our dear friends. I told her to shop smart and be generous with her money.

Do we really need this stuff we are buying? Does your friend or family member need Jesus? Do they need prayer today . . . a bold prayer that will shape their eternity? Can Black Friday be something more than stuff?

Loving you all today! Loved my and Bridget's photo shoot yesterday so I thought I would share another. 😊

November 25 at 7:37 a.m.
Saturday

My kids

I wanted four kids . . . three boys and one girl . . . and that is exactly what God gave me in four and half years. It was a crazy time . . . but like the best time ever. Knee deep in diapers was where I wanted to be. Look at the fruits of that blessing. Four healthy, God-loving children.

I am thankful today for them and for those who help me raise them . . . my husband . . . teachers at school . . . our family members . . . our friends (who will just pick them up and take them places . . . this amazes me).

God is great! My prayer is that these kids are on fire for Jesus . . . that they speak audaciously about the Lord to whoever needs to hear it . . . that they are a light to the darkness.

Happy Saturday!

November 26 at 8:04 a.m.
Sunday Funday

*M*y goal is to give all of you some encouragement before you are on your way to wherever it may be. I was thinking about church . . . We are the church, but hopefully you belong to a local church? I never knew how important the local body was until all of this happened. They are my family . . . they love me . . . check in on me all the time . . . give me cards and encouragement every day. We couldn't do what we do here without them.

I hear all the time "I love Jesus, but I don't like those Christians" . . . well . . . I understand that, but we all fail and we all need Jesus to get things right . . . and even then . . . things don't go right.

My people are at Perkiomenville Mennonite Church and they are our family . . . Where are your people? Find people! It will bless you and your family. Don't throw Jesus out with the "Christians" . . . don't make "Christians" a bad word . . . the world made that bad for you . . . come on back! 😊

November 27 at 7:50 a.m.
Monday

God is moving in this world even though we don't see it or feel it . . . it is something I cling to every morning. I read the book of Ecclesiastes just the other day . . . Talk about showing you really what you're working towards . . . We do so much, and the end result is "smoke" (Message translation). But . . . God is there and moving . . . He sets Eternity in our hearts.

> "The Maker of heaven and earth embedded deep within the human psyche an innate suspicion that He is out there. We can silence it of course it takes a fair amount of commitment to keep it silent. More often it whispers in the quiet when we are alone, and it squirms in the stillness when we have got no place to go." ~Beth Moore
>
> The question today is . . . what are you going to do with Jesus? Move with Him and take part in what He is doing in your life even in the little things? Or are you going to just make this a "normal" day?

Who can you bless today . . . who can you pray for? Can you pray for the Egyptians who are suffering? Can you pray for your neighbor who you may not know that well? Let's make today more than cyber Monday (I say this because my phone is constantly ringing right now with so many deals for stuff I literally do not need) . . . Let's give today to our God, who is on the move. Hallelujah! 😊

November 28 at 6:05 a.m.
Tuesday

*I*t's so early and the sun hasn't come up yet, but I know that God has this day . . . every part . . . do you? Can you trust that He isn't going to let you down today, even though sometimes it definitely feels like He dropped the ball with what is going on in your life? Jesus loves us so much, and it is something that we can hardly fathom. Our most important commandment is to love the Lord (Mark 12:28). This is the most important . . . love the Lord your God with all your heart, with all your soul, with all your mind, and with all your strength.

> "This love Jesus longs for is not just devotion. It's also an emotion. It's not just volition. It's also affection. It's is not just discipline. It's also a passion. It's not just routine. It's a romance . . . and not just for Christ's sake but also for ours" ~ Beth Moore

Love Him today by serving Him . . . my question each morning is: how am I going to serve Jesus? And that was never on my radar before . . . Who can I talk to today . . . pray for today . . . hug today that is going to bless them more than you would know? I would love to know anything that you need me to pray for.

P.S. I am watching the news right now and saw this man who is blind and was beaten at the 69th Street El station. Lord. help us to be ready to love everyone. 😊

November 29 at 5:35 a.m.
Wednesday

Hi, friends.

I am here just thinking and praying for the day and what it may bring.

Yesterday God brought a good friend back into my life, and it was such a blessing talking with her and catching up. During this time of reconnection, we remembered some of the bad things that happened in our relationship that made us run far from one another . . .

This makes me want to just gather all those people that I have not been talking to . . . and talk to them. If I have been distant or cruel . . . please, I am so very sorry. I love and appreciate you all and I really want to be used by the Lord to pray for you and to be your friend.

Romans 15:5–6: "May the God who gives endurance and encouragement give you the same attitude of mind toward each other that Christ Jesus had so that with one mind and one voice you may glorify the God and Father of our Lord Jesus Christ."

Have a wonderful Wednesday. Be a blessing by just giving a smile or a hug. If you are in need of prayer . . . please reach out. Thank you all for the dinners and delicious things you keep making our family . . . it's been amazing.

*B*eing from where I come from comes with a mouth that sometimes is not filtered . . . in a good way too. Philly girls will tell you their feelings . . . you never have to wonder. Today you're not going to have to wonder.

Jesus loves you . . . loves you more than I can describe to you . . . words do no good describing this love. There are so many Bible references that describe this love . . . Old Testament and New Testament (God is unchangeable, so if you hear that He changes in the New Testament . . . that is a lie!).

We know Adam and Eve had one command . . . "Don't eat of that tree" . . . We know Satan tempted them . . . trying to make them the "gods" of their lives . . . we know the end result. But . . . an amazing gift was promised that day . . . Jesus. And through the Old Testament you see Jesus coming.

Being in Advent season . . . this is where Jesus comes . . . He came of His own free will . . . born in a filthy stable where it was cold and disgusting from a teenage mom who was scared and felt unworthy. He did this for you and me . . . expecting nothing from us. He came to give us the free gift of salvation. His death on the cross at Easter is the payment for the bad things that we do every day . . . it takes away our sins and washes us clean so that when we go to meet our Savior we can live with Him forever in heaven. It's a free gift! You don't have to earn it, and there is no way you could, so why try?

It's a bit like this . . . you are married, but every night your husband comes home and checks your work . . . Did you clean well? Are the kids well behaved? This is all on you, Mom! If you don't get your husband's approval, you are out! Is this love? No! This is the kind of love some of us are living under every day. You can't earn Jesus's love . . . it's free! Take it!

John 3:16–17: "For God so loved the world that He gave His only Son, that whoever believes in Him shall not perish but have eternal life. For God did not send the Son in the world to judge the world but that the world might be saved through Him."

He came for you! Had you on His heart . . . He's still searching for you . . . don't miss it by jumping through hoops here on earth . . . It's a free gift! Take it . . . Merry Christmas!

If you have any questions . . . I'm here!

December 1 at 5:36 a.m.
Friday

You made it through the week, friends . . . congratulations!

I wanted to talk about prayer. So often we say, "I'll pray for you," and we completely forget. That is just part of our humanity . . . we forget stuff all the time. Last night we had some precious friends visiting and going to God was just what was required . . . nothing else would do . . . so we prayed right then and there. It was a wonderful display of God's comfort and power. Try this for me today . . . stop and pray . . . don't wait . . . let God know that you need Him right then.

This is something I didn't do . . . my whole life . . . but now I talk to Jesus first . . . He understands me even when I have no words . . . He wants us to cry out to Him and then be still and wait for Him to move!

The Bible verse that came through a minute ago is the verse that is on my wall here in my office at home (I call it my "take your wife to work" place).

Exodus 14:14: "The Lord will fight for you, you need only to be still. He's fighting while you're praying and then you just wait."

Have a great Friday . . . keep praying . . . and keep sending me things you would like me to pray for . . . I have time and would love to partner with you in prayer. 🐨

December 2 at 9:34 a.m.
Saturday

*G*ood morning and sorry that I didn't post this morning right away. I am reading a Max Lucado book called *In the Manger*. This is what spoke to me today.

Immanuel (God with us) . . . Why would He come?

Philippians 2:6–7: Christ Himself was like God in everything . . . but He gave up his place with God and made Himself nothing, He was born as a man and became like a servant.

The God of our universe willing was born into poverty . . . spent His first night willingly in a cow's feeding trough . . . He did it eyes wide open, when He could've said "No!" Why? Because He loves being with the ones He loves!

Story (borrowing from Max Lucado):

A plastic surgeon named Dr. Maxwell Maltz tells the story of a man who had been burned in a fire trying to save his parents, but he couldn't get to them and they died in the fire. He thought his pain was God's punishment. His face was disfigured, and he would let no one see him, not even his wife. His wife went to the doctor and asked him to disfigure her face in the same way and this would show her love for him and she would be let back in his life. The surgeon told the man of his wife's desire to be like him and the man opened the door and let her in.

Do you see the love? The way the woman felt about her husband is a fraction . . . just a fraction of the way Jesus loves us . . . He took our face and was willing to be like us . . . He loves to be with the ones He loves!

That is Christmas! Don't miss it . . . tell others! Show others! 😊

December 3 at 9:36 a.m.
Sunday

*R*eally prayed about what to share today . . . really, really . . . I pray right now that it blesses you in whatever you are doing.

2 Corinthians 5:14–15 (The Message):

> Our firm decision is to work from this focused center: one man died for everyone. That puts everyone in the same boat. He included everyone in his death so that we could be included in his life, a resurrection life, a far better life than people ever lived on their own.

Two questions . . . What are you most compelled by the love of Christ to do? What would it take to do it?

Love is the catalyst . . . the cause and effect!

When Christ's love invades every cell in your body . . . that's where the rubber meets the road!

What are you going to do today? Don't waste it . . . pray boldly . . . speak love to a family member that you may not be loving like you should. Think differently about Christmas and celebrating it . . . Do something today because Jesus loves you and died for you. Don't waste it!

I'm praying for you.

Have a wonderful Sunday. 😊

December 4 at 6:34 a.m.
Monday

$\mathcal{F}$orgiveness is the theme that I landed on this morning . . . what the Holy Spirit helped me land on.

My posture for years has been flight or fight . . . mostly flight. I run protection mode for me and for my immediate family.

This morning I was reading about Joseph and his life being a picture of Christ.

Genesis 45:7–8: "God sent me on ahead to pave the way and make way and make sure there was a remnant in the land to save your lives in an amazing act of deliverance. So you see, it wasn't you who sent me but God. He set me in place as a father to Pharaoh, put me in charge of his personal affairs, and made me ruler of all Egypt."

What would you have done if it were you? I know . . . those brothers and family would never see me again. God had another plan that brought God glory and redemption to a family.

My story is not similar to this in every way . . . but it is miraculous . . . God has brought amazing reconciliation to our family and love that sustains us every day. God can do that in your lives. Reach out today . . . Don't let forgiveness and reconciliation pass you by, because that is God's story.

Mercy Me: "If I told you my story, you would hear hope that wouldn't let go. If I told you my story, you would hear love that never gave up. If I told you my story, you would hear life, but it wasn't mine."

If you could pray for our family . . . we just got news that our beloved grandmother died a few hours ago . . . Bob's grandmom Ruth Wolfe (1920–2017). We know she's in a better place where she can experience that reconciliation and redemption . . . she's at the feet of Jesus. 😏

December 5 at 6:05 a.m.
Tuesday

My advent reading was about Ruth and Naomi and the love that Ruth showed Naomi even when Naomi saw bitterness and blackness because she lost her sons and her husband. She named herself *Mara* meaning "bitter."

Ruth 1:16–17: But Ruth said, "Don't force me to leave you, don't make me go home. Where you go, I go and where you live, I'll live. Your people are my people, your God is my God: where you die I'll die, and that's where I'll be buried, so help me God . . . not even death itself is going to come between us!"

This is an amazing action by this young woman. She put her mother-in-law ahead of her own comfort . . . like forever . . . it's in convenient language . . . a promise that she intended to keep.

She meets Boaz, and God makes that marriage happen and redeems the whole situation . . . Boaz is the kinsman redeemer. In Hebrew law, the kinsman redeemer is the male relative and who had the privilege to act on behalf of a relative who was in trouble . . . he delivers and rescues.

Jesus is our kinsman redeemer . . . ! Believe this is a great focus for us during this season of advent . . . Christmas is the story that Jesus redeems . . . He's redeeming things every day. Are you taking things to him? He's the ultimate redeemer. Before you try to fix something . . . give it to Jesus right away. I think that is what Ruth did . . . she just decided to love and stay. Can you do that? Love and stay and let

Jesus redeem. Let go of all the stuff and give it to Jesus! He's waiting for you!

Have a wonderful Tuesday.

Praying for you.

December 6 at 5:56 a.m.
Wednesday

*B*oldness!

Let's do it . . . be bold . . . be bold in your prayers . . . be bold in your love . . . be bold in service . . . be audaciously bold.

I think we are scared to just say it . . . stop being scared and give it to God.

There are so many passages in Scripture (especially in Acts) where the apostles were bold, and that boldness advanced the kingdom of God. Can you advance the kingdom of God today by being bold? Is there something or someone today that needs boldness? God is working through you and will continue.

I love the story of Ruth not only for the redemption story that points directly to Jesus . . . but because she has boldness . . . She was going to stay with Naomi no matter what Naomi had to say . . . she didn't care. The courage and boldness she had to stay with her kind of bitter mother-in-law is amazing to me . . .

God made you to use this day for His Glory . . . How are you going to do that? Don't waste it! God is doing miracles! We have stories . . . God is moving, and He wants you to be bold!

I'm praying for you!

Happy Bold Wednesday!

*G*et out of that boat!

In Matthew 14 we have the true biblical account of Peter and the disciples in the boat waiting for Jesus to be done praying on the mountain. The boat that the disciples had was beaten by the waves and the winds were howling. The disciples were afraid. Jesus comes walking on the sea between 3:00 through 6:00 a.m. . . . (Jesus doesn't need dry land from a great wind . . . He just comes). Everyone is afraid except that Simon Peter . . . He says, "If You are (God . . . literally I Aм) can I come?" And Jesus's response is "Yes, come ahead!"

We know what happens to Peter, and it would probably happen to many of us . . . We fear . . . we cry out . . . God rescues. Peter has the ultimate experienced faith . . . He gets out of the boat with nothing to hold on to . . . he just goes . . . He could have enjoyed God in the boat like the rest of them . . . but not Peter!

When Jesus commands us to GO . . . He is going to get us there no matter what miracle it's going to take!

Daniel 11:32b: "But the people who know their God shall be strong and carry out great exploits!"

The Bible is full of these promises. What's your destination today? Are you going to get out of the boat like Peter, who did it like there was nothing to lose? He already denied the Lord three times . . . He wanted Jesus badly, so he did whatever it took . . .

Stay in the boat? Or follow Jesus?

Have a great Thursday. ☕

33

December 8 at 6:11 a.m.
Friday

*H*ope: cherishing a desire with anticipation, to want something to happen or to be true.

I was reading about the demon-possessed man who was messed up . . . They did things to help this man who lived among the tombs . . . bound him with chains to help him and protect him from himself. Didn't work.

Jesus gets off the boat after calming the sea and He is met immediately with our friend. Can you identify with this man?

> He needed HELP!
> He needed shelter.
> He needed a miracle!

So the demons talked to Jesus and asked to be driven into the pigs. They called him the Son of the Most High God. This is who we put our trust in . . . the Savior of the World . . . more people than the spiritual forces we fight against every day!

So . . . many came to see the end result . . . this guy is now "clean" and in his right mind! Miracle!

Have you ever felt:

> Insane?
> Irrational?
> Out of control?
> Life chaotic?

Jesus creates BEAUTY FROM ASHES (Isaiah 61:3).

He gives us a right mind and a clear vision.

He gives us peace because He is the prince of peace.

We are a NEW creation.

Jesus is working during this advent season, and we can find our hope in Christ . . . God sent the Savior to REDEEM all mankind through His life, death, and resurrection.

That is our hope . . . Jesus is our Hope, our living hope!

Go today boldly knowing that you have a hope . . . living . . . eternal and powerful! It brings freedom to your life if you let it. Don't waste today . . . spread that hope to others.

Love and prayers to all of you. Please let me know if you need prayer . . . I'm here, my friends.

Have a wonderful Friday.

December 9 at 7:20 a.m.
Saturday

Full restoration.

*S*halom: completeness, wholeness, health peace, welfare, safety, soundness, perfectness, rest, absence of agitation or discord. There's a modern Hebrew word, *shelem*, which means "to fully pay for." There is only one way for full SHALOM and that is Yahweh . . . He is the only way we can have true peace, contentment, and that exhaustive list I have compiled above.

Today's reading is about the woman with the issue of blood that made He unclean for twelve years. This biblical account is what I held on to during my few months with chronic pain . . . I just kept saying that I would touch His clothes . . . I believe!

This woman was desperate for healing and for release from shame!

Matthew 9: Just then a woman who had hemorrhages for twelve years slipped behind and gently touched his robe . . . Jesus turned and caught her at it and reassured her . . . "Courage, daughter, you took a risk and you are well!"

In an instant she was healed! He immediately healed her and called her daughter, which was never done before. I don't want to leave the men out, but girls . . . he called her daughter. You are the daughter of the Most High!

In the Old Testament they longed for Jesus and Shalom . . .

Now: we have access to Jesus in every moment of every day through prayer, Bible study . . . being with those who love Jesus too!

Do you long to touch Jesus and for Him to give you full restoration? The woman in the passage was now clean, she had a full restoration/redemption . . . a whole healing . . .

You can have that today . . . don't waste it. Ask for that Shalom, and no matter the circumstances around you . . . God's going to work through you like this precious daughter who had amazing faith in a Jesus that she had only heard stories about.

If you are praying this morning . . . can you pray that I able to get into the car and go to the celebration of our precious grandmother without pain? We know God can do anything, so we are trusting that it will be fine . . . but prayer warriors certainly help!

Have a wonderful Saturday in the snow? 😎

A bit late today . . . got a little chance to sleep in. Thanks for you for your prayers yesterday . . . we were able to enjoy our time as a family and celebrate an amazing life lived for Jesus to its fullest!

Adultery is certainly not a Sunday morning topic . . . but forgiveness and sin are always topics that we should address. Sin is for sure on fire in this world. It. It makes us not want to watch the news or interact with those we know are "bad."

Jesus is at the temple . . . and the Pharisees are hot on His trail to get Him . . . to catch Him in sin because that was what they focused on . . . the Law . . . not the glorious freedom Jesus offered from that Law . . . the fulfillment JESUS was to the Law.

The woman was alone. The man that she was caught with was gone and out of shame's sight. She was alone in front of everyone. She had no court of law to defend her . . . she was just alone. Except for Jesus. He writes in the dirt. We don't know what Jesus was writing in the dirt, but we do know that Jesus was emphasizing that no one can judge because we all have sinned and fallen short. He turned the tables on their plans to get Jesus and get this woman.

Jesus forgave this woman without condition, BUT he didn't leave her without direction . . . "Go and sin no more." Jesus's forgiveness teaches us to live differently . . . liberates us to live differently! Jesus loved this woman and the one at the well. He gave them a new life which included a direction to live differently . . . live without sinning (not possible, but worth a life of giving yourself to others, to loving others, etc.).

We need to tell people that Jesus loves them, but He wants us to read and follow Scriptures . . . to read and follow God's Word. Surprisingly those in our churches are taking Jesus's love and making that something that we should be concerned with ONLY . . . and Jesus's love is what wakes me up in the morning . . . but we have to live in the tension of Jesus's love and the truth of the gospel. Do you have the courage to do both? Jesus went to the well . . . loved this daughter but told her it was time to clean up her life. There's a lot in the Bible that is tough and hard, and we don't want to do it . . . or we know people who may be doing what is wrong and living that way . . . the Bible is clear . . . we need to follow God's word!

Beth Moore: "You will watch a generation of Christians set their Bible aside in attempt to become more like Jesus . . . and stunningly it will sound completely plausible. This will be perhaps the cleverest of all the devil's schemes in your generation . . . sacrifice truth for Love's sake and you will rise or fall based on whether you will sacrifice one for the other. Will you have the courage to live in the tension of both truth and love?"

Lots to think about on Sunday.

December 11 at 6:20 a.m.
Monday

*H*ave you ever said, "I don't get it"? I said this several times yesterday because my cousin came all the way from Texas to see me, and in my family, I am the youngest grandchild out of nine grandchildren . . . in some cases, I'm twenty years younger than my cousins . . . they live all over the country, and the only way to see them is on Facebook or a funeral. But God has been doing so much restoration and reconciliation here that I guess I get it.

Sometimes things are just complicated: consisting of parts. intricately combined and difficult to analyze understand or explain . . . but Jesus is untying those things that are knotted and which we can't necessarily explain.

The mustard seed parable is one that everyone knows. The farmer throws the seed and forgets about it. The seed grows without his help at all . . . it ripens . . . it's fully formed . . . it's harvest time.

God's kingdom is upside down . . . This little mustard seed is the faith it takes to advance the kingdom. Jesus is using you to advance this kingdom if you allow Him to work in your life and you have not only the faith of the mustard seed but you're planting seeds. That neighbor you talked to yesterday and mentioned Jesus to . . . follow up with that conversation. Plant and water that seed . . . pray that the seed will grow.

Sidenote: I love that Jesus explained things to the disciples. Mark 4:33-34: "With many stories like these, he presented his message to them, lifting the stories to their

41

experience and maturity. He was never without a story when he spoke. When he was alone with his disciples, he went over everything, sorting out the tangles, untying the knots."

Jesus, untangle our knots today! Bring people in our lives that need seeds planted and watered. Bring us people who need Jesus and His good news . . . It's not complicated! He loves you . . . came to earth to die for you . . . rose again so you can have eternal life . . . not complicated!

I am really praying for you . . . because I love you and I know that Jesus is answering these requests. Saturday's outing was Jesus answering prayers all day long . . .

Getting in the 🌑
Getting out of the 🌑
Bathroom.
New wheelchair that was able to go down
steps.
Eating.
Etc. . . .
All these little prayers were answered.

So . . . Look what God is doing . . . it's not me . . . all glory goes to Him . . . All!
Have a wonderful Monday! 🌑

*H*ealing . . . a theme that I am exploring now, and really the theme of advent . . . a time of anticipation of what Jesus is doing . . . He came to earth to heal us.

The disciples see this blind man at the gate who is a second-class citizen because he cannot support himself so day after day he sits at the temple gate and asks for charity (food, money, etc.). The disciples weren't interested in the blind man . . . they were interested in the why he was blind . . . they were being judgmental . . . Jesus was focusing on physical and spiritual healing.

Jesus put mud on the man's eyes and instructed him to wash in the pool of Siloam. The man was questioned by the Jews at the temple . . . He didn't back down . . . He told them that Jesus was a prophet and openly worshipped Him without fear.

His spiritual eyes were opened . . . Have your eyes been opened today? Jesus is the Messiah and your identity's in Christ! He's your light . . .

Are you trying hard in your own strength (which seems like the American way)? I worked hard today . . . I really had success today, because I stayed at work late and accomplished something. Our works are like filthy rags . . . they will maybe get us somewhere on earth . . . but Jesus wants your heart. Jesus wants you to concentrate on people that He wants you to love . . . He wants you to see the reconciliation and redemption He offers, and He wants you to not only GO and tell but stay with that seed and water it every day . . . Prayer goes a long way. Accomplish things today for the kingdom . . . the kingdom of God is what matters. Stuff doesn't. Is God speaking to you right now? Listen to that still small voice . . . that's the Holy Spirit . . .

John 9:25: He replied, "I know nothing about that one way or another, but one thing I know for sure, I was blind I now see."

Seek the Savior and you'll never be blind again. 😊

*C*omplications and simplifications.

This is the third time that I have tried to type this and get it on the update. I feel under attack by the devil. He doesn't want you to see this for some reason. He wants life and its complications to make you ineffective today. God may have someone in your path that needs your love and your life-giving words from Jesus today and he doesn't want you to share them.

Jesus is victory . . . His plan for you is a simple one . . . love others and serve Him.

2 Corinthians 4:8: "We are afflicted in every way but not crushed, we are perplexed but not driven to despair."

Here's some simple truths for today:

1. Life is complicated.
2. Jesus is the master at untying knots and whatever is holding you back . . . ask Him to lead you today.
3. Today has a purpose . . . it's not just about making money at your job . . . there's more . . . look for the more . . . look for the person who needs Jesus . . . look for the person who seems to be in pain . . . LOOK.
4. God raises unlikely heroes (read Philippians 1) . . . you can be that hero of the faith . . .
5. Get past your past! God is redeeming and restoring you! Let Him.

6. Seek God's kingdom . . . because you can't beat a deal like Jesus!

Have a great day and after three times trying to post this . . . I hope it's a great day finding ways to serve the Lord. Remember to LOOK!

Outside the cross of Jesus Christ, there is no hope in this world. That cross and resurrection at the core of the Gospel is the only hope for humanity. Wherever you go, ask God for wisdom on how to get that Gospel in, even in the toughest situations of life.

*H*appy two-hour delay! My kids are quietly enjoying the extra sleep. This morning I read a few accounts of the rich young ruler and his desire to earn eternal life. His questions were just what you would expect from someone who had abounding knowledge of the Law. He did everything that he was supposed to do . . . everything. When Jesus asked him to give up all he had he couldn't do it.

His life was caught up in stuff . . . he couldn't surrender and follow Jesus because that stuff defined him. In fact, in one of the accounts Jesus described the process . . . it would be easier for a camel to go through the eye of a needle . . . something that I would love to see. Jesus says, "With man it is impossible, but with God all things are possible."

The amazing and extremely happy *fact* is that we don't need to do anything to ensure eternal life . . . it's a free gift (Ephesians 2:8–9) that we don't have earn . . . but with that free gift we will want to surrender our human stuff . . . our hustle and bustle . . . wealth . . . things that we can't live without (seemingly).

Our family is cleaning out our grandmother's apartment. Being ninety-seven years old . . . you can imagine the amount of things . . . papers . . . furniture . . . jewelry, etc. She couldn't take anything to heaven with her . . . here it sits . . . there's the proof . . . this stuff is just stuff, and you can't take it with you.

Today . . . what can we surrender to Jesus and make Him Lord? That trip to Kohl's? Do you need to buy that loofa? Do you need to stay late at work tonight? Do you need to ignore that phone call from your neighbor? Can you give up something and make Jesus reign? Can you pray right now and give today to Jesus? Every minute . . . surrender your weakness to Him and make Him your strength! This surrender will give freedom and joy! Go tell others . . . they will see it in your life, but don't be afraid to tell others. Go shout it on that mountaintop!

December 15 at 6:22 a.m.
Friday

*W*e made it . . . sigh of huge relief.

Today's devotion led me to Zacchaeus. Thankfully a story that all children know and can even sing a song about to tell you the redemptive work Jesus did for someone hated by his peers. I sometimes wonder who the fellow Jews actually liked, because they were so pitted against each other.

He was disliked for his abuse of the tax system but seemed ready to make some restitution to those he wronged. He was a short guy, couldn't see, but found the appropriate tree and hoisted his smallness up there because he wasn't going to miss Jesus! What happened next was probably so crazy to all that maybe everyone was stunned silent . . . Jesus called him by *name*! "I'm going to your house today, Zacchaeus" . . . dinner and fellowship. Zacchaeus welcomes the Savior of the world!

Zacchaeus recognizes his sin to the people and offers half his possessions and four times more to those he cheated. He was ready to make right a situation!

2 Corinthians 5:17: "If anyone believes in Christ He is a new creation. The Old has passed away and the new has come."

Jesus is searching for you by name. He knew you . . . chose you. This is the message of Christmas. Zacchaeus was a sinner . . . one that the Jews thought one of the worst . . . Jesus wants to have dinner with this man . . . He chose him and redeemed his life. It's simple. We make things so complicated and difficult. He knows your name . . . He chose you. He chose you not to keep it silent . . . don't keep it to yourself . . . make disciples, and that means getting out there . . . talking to people who don't necessarily know.

I know the name of Santa makes folks who are God-fearing like invoking the name of Satan . . . but Santa got out there . . . St. Nicholas gave of himself quietly and helped all those who needed food and I am sure he prayed for them . . . he gave time and himself to those who had very little. He loved the Lord and showed that. Of course, the world has made this Santa someone we go to and tell our wants for Christmas and make Christmas about stuff. I say we take that back too . . . redeem that story about St. Nick. If you dive further in his real story, you'll see more stuff to like about this man.

Have a wonderful Friday . . . cold but full of Jesus's great love!

December 16 at 11:27 a.m.
Saturday

Good morning, friends . . . better late than never, I had some extra time to sleep this morning and I took advantage of that.

I just wanted to run through all that Jesus was showing me this week from the true biblical accounts.

Jesus brings PEACE. We lack peace because we look for God's presence in other places and fill our souls with stuff.

Inner turmoil comes from sin . . . and that sin turns to panic . . . but we learn from the woman that Jesus comes into contact with, that no sin is unforgivable, and the woman caught in sin must have been so happy to enjoy God's peace through mercy and grace.

Healer . . . Jesus heals us spiritually and physically, and this brings peace to us . . .

Possessions . . . stuff does not bring peace. The anxiety you feel when you don't have a present for that person who may be getting you something. You feel nervous that you have to reciprocate . . . that is not peace!

Generosity is true peace and freedom . . . serving others means you have a transformed heart . . .

We have the Holy Spirit living inside us and that helps us be open to everyday encounters with Jesus Christ. Don't miss Him in the distractions of today . . . Don't miss the true peace He offers when we trust in Him.

Exodus 14:14: "The Lord will fight for you . . . you need only to be still."

John 14:27: "Peace, I leave with you my peace, not as the world gives do I give to you, let not your hearts be troubled, neither let them be afraid."

Surrender is the theme really anchored in these true biblical accounts . . . open your hands and let go . . . God will bless that surrender to Him. He will show you His grace and mercy . . . His Holy Spirit will guide you and comfort you.

Have a wonderful day today.

December 17 at 7:29 a.m.
Sunday

*G*ood morning, friends. I am in the throes of not really knowing what to write, but I know the Lord is working right now. I am listening to "Silent Night" and thinking about those teenagers in that stable delivering the Son of God . . . and the shepherds seeing the angels . . . the angels telling the lowest of the low about the highest of the high . . . Jesus Christ!

During this time, I have been at home recovering from my almost-three-week hospital stay. I have seen God move in so many ways it is hard to describe it all to you. I have seen my husband as a true picture of Christ. On a typical day we get up at 5:00 a.m. and he gives me all my medication and then gets right up to shower and help the kids get out of the house. He goes straight on to helping me get washed and dressed . . . coffee and breakfast . . . vacuuming all my hair that still insists on falling out. That is just a picture of what he does. I am getting stronger but still need him. He has now included getting me out of the house to go to dinner, and today CHURCH.

Beth Moore started a study of Philemon (one-chapter book in the New Testament) which is about a slave named Onesimus who ran away. His name means "useless." He was a runaway slave of Philemon, and Paul wants Philemon to take him back because he has become so useful and is ready to serve not only as a slave but as brother in Christ. Slavery is a tough topic now and back then. That is a study for another time.

He wanted to be useful and serve others! Philemon and Onesimus, slave owner and slave . . . had no idea that believing in Jesus would involve social change . . . they were brought together because they followed Jesus. They loved Jesus. Who will come into your life because you love Jesus? How can you show Jesus's love today? Can you serve someone today?

I did much blabbering today and I don't really know where I went with this post, but the Holy Spirit put every part in my heart.

Have a wonderful Sunday, and if that takes you to church . . . enjoy the fellowship . . . If you are at home . . . enjoy something . . . Find a sermon with worship online . . . There is so much to choose from . . . Make sure God's Word is used! ☺

*J*esus is pursuing you right now in this dark and chilly Monday before Christmas.

He's chosen you! First John 4:19 is a great verse to help you remember that He loves us first!

Jesus doesn't love us like we love ourselves, which is love yourself and then hate yourself.

- Jesus isn't moody.
- Jesus loves eternally and infinitely.
- Jesus loves fiery and feverishly.
- Jesus loves audaciously.

I have been studying Israel and their disobedience . . . sometimes just slight disobedience . . . they would do some of what they were supposed to . . . which led to consequences down the road. God never left them . . . even though they were doing what was right in their own eyes (Judges 21:25).

Here's an abbreviated list of Israel's behavior and ways God brought them back!

The Law was given.
Rebellion in the wilderness.
Forty years wandering and many not making it to the promised land (Moses).
Joshua crosses the Jordan.
Entered the land of "milk and honey."

Giants in the land.
Judges rose up to lead.
Judges were followed by kings.
King David was a man after God's own heart.

Jesus said in 2 Samuel 7:16, "Your house and kingdom will endure before me forever and your throne will be established forever."

David dies . . . sons die . . . kingdom divided and carried into several captivities.

Prophets rose . . . told the people to go back to God.

Amos 8:11: "Hear this! The days are coming—this is the declaration of the Lord God . . . when I will send a famine though the land not a famine of bread or a thirst for water, but of the hearing of the Word of the Lord."

SILENCE. For four generations.
So, after that list, which I hope didn't put you to sleep . . . Christmas!
God's redemption! He chose you!
The angels had problems understanding this plan.
Colossians 2:9: ". . . For in Him all the fullness of the deity was made complete."
Jesus . . .
Turned water into wine.
Cleansed lepers.
Healed the sick.
Loved children.
Gave sight to the blind.

Gave hearing to the deaf.
Confounded those wise temple friends.
Called everyone to follow Him.
Dined with sinners.
Cursed the fig tree.
Rode a donkey.
Cast out demons.
Fed thousands.
Raised the dead!

So . . . What do we do with Jesus? Put away your shame . . . pray that He can use you not only this Christmas but every day. Jesus loves you with this audacious love that we can't measure . . . but you can talk to others and give it away. You are outrageously loved, and there's no shame in that!

I know that this post is long, but I wanted you all to see that through all the disobedience from Israel . . . God still loves . . . He forgives you no matter what . . . I used to say this every morning to my little preschoolers. There is nothing you can do to make God angry . . . He loves you no matter what! No matter what! Accept that forgiveness!

Forgiveness is freedom!

Have a wonderful Monday (which doesn't go together in our minds, but can you make Monday awesome with the news of Jesus and His redemption where HE CHOSE YOU)!

I'm praying for you. 😊

*G*ood morning, my friends. I see from my son's clothes that the weather is going to be a bit warmer, because he is wearing shorts . . . Who needs a weather forecast when you have a sixteen-year-old?

Focusing on time today . . . every morning I wake up and look at my calendar and see who is coming to visit or who will be coming tomorrow . . . It is exciting, and it also focuses how I am going to pray. I think we are all focused on time this week as Christmas is right around the comer and we have to get ready for the big day. Can we instead today focus on Jesus and His heart and His Word . . . and getting that Word out to those who need it so desperately but may not show it?

I wanted to focus on 1 Timothy 6:3–10: "If anyone advocates a different doctrine and does not agree with sound words, those of our Lord Jesus Christ, and with the doctrine conforming to godliness . . . he is conceited and understands nothing; but he has a morbid interest in controversial questions and disputes about words, out of which arise envy, strife, abusive language, evil suspicions, and constant friction between men of depraved mind and deprived of the truth, who suppose that godliness is a means of gain. But godliness actually is a means of great gain when accompanied by contentment. For we have brought nothing into the world, so we cannot take anything out of it either. If we have food and covering, with these we shall be content. But those who want to get rich fail into temptation and a snare and many foolish and harmful desires which plunge men into ruin and destruction. For the love of money is a root of all sorts of evil, and some by longing for it have wandered away from the faith and pierced themselves with many griefs."

Let's not deprive ourselves of truth while in the pursuit of anything else. We want to fight the good fight and bring people to Jesus this Christmas season. Bring people to Jesus's great love.

Our family has so many people blessing us . . . it is a beautiful sight to see every day, and we just can't believe it. The word "deserve" pops in my head every time someone calls/texts/emails us to bless us. We don't deserve anything if we are working in our own "good works" . . . praise the Lord that His gifts are fully without merit . . . because I can't be good enough to merit anything.

Bring them in today . . . bring people to Jesus today . . . before that four-letter word TIME gets too late. Never fear talking about JESUS, because He goes before and behind you and will never let you go . . . or leave you alone.

You know I would love to pray for you today . . . please let me know how I can! God is good and continues to bless. He is doing miracles here in the Hadden household . . . He has restored strength to my arm that was literally numb . . . I had to pick it up with my other hand . . . that's how numb it was. He has brought the swelling down in my knee and foot . . . and they are looking normal. He has allowed me to go to church, visit a friend, go out to dinner, see Christmas lights, ride along to take my son to a Christmas party. He has allowed me to be alert and awake and enjoy my time with my family. He has brought amazing people in my life and allowed me to redeem the time with those that I "wrote off" years ago. Your prayers are being answered, and I am so blessed by all of you, I am trying to write personalized thank-yous so you know just how grateful we are.

Have a wonderful Tuesday!

December 20 at 6:38 a.m.
Wednesday

Good morning, my friends. I hope that you are looking forward to a great day! Christmas is only a few days
away and the craziness of that can make us wake up to
anxiety and stress . . . Put that away if you can right now
and give that to God.

Our family has been dealing with some pretty strong
spiritual attacks . . . times where we are upset and having
arguments about things that really don't matter . . . strong
attacks. We know our God is greater!

I want to focus on Hebrews 12:18–29:

"For you have not come to a mountain that can be
touched and to a blazing fire, and to darkness and gloom
and whirlwind, and to the blast of a trumpet and the sound
of words which sound was such that those who heard
begged that no further word be spoken to them. For they
could not bear the command, 'IF EVEN A BEAST TOUCHES
THE MOUNTAIN, IT WILL BE STONED.' And so terrible was the
sight, that Moses said, 'I am full of fear and trembling.' But
you have come to Mount Zion and to the city of the living
God, the heavenly Jerusalem, and to myriads of angels, to
the general assembly and church of the firstborn who are
enrolled in heaven, and to God, the Judge of all, and to
the spirits of the righteous made perfect, and to Jesus, the
mediator of a new covenant, and to the sprinkled blood,
which speaks better than the blood of Abel. See to it that
you do not refuse Him who is speaking. For if those did
not escape when they refused him who warned them on

earth, much less will we escape who turn away from Him who warns from heaven. And His voice shook the earth then, but now He has promised, saying, 'YET ONCE MORE I WILL SHAKE NOT ONLY THE EARTH, BUT ALSO THE HEAVEN.'"

This expression, "Yet once more," denotes the removing of those things which can be shaken, as of created things, so that those things which cannot be shaken may remain. Therefore, since we receive a kingdom which cannot be shaken, let us show gratitude, by which we may offer to God an acceptable service with reverence.

Date: Thu, Dec 21, 2017 6:27 am

Good morning, friends! It's so dark this morning. It's the winter solstice today. Every morning I wake up at five and take my prescribed medication and go into God's Word. This is something that I am so happy to do because for so many years the Word of God was on the very back burner or not even there at all. Sure, I knew the Word, but I didn't read it and get that fire in my bones from its power. There is power in the Word!

I wanted to show you some verses that describe that power of God's Word . . . and the calling that comes from God's Word!

Here we have Isaiah 6:1–9:

> In the year of King Uzziah's death I saw the Lord sitting on a throne, lofty and exalted, with the train of His robe filling the temple. Seraphim stood above Him, each having six wings: with two he covered his face, and with two he covered his feet, and with two he flew. And one called out to another and said, "Holy, Holy, Holy, is the LORD of hosts, the whole earth is full of His glory." And the foundations of the thresholds trembled at the voice of him who called out, while the temple was filling with smoke. Then I said, "Woe is me, for I am ruined! Because I am a man of unclean lips, And I live among a people

of unclean lips; For my eyes have seen the King, the LORD of hosts." Then one of the seraphim flew to me with a burning coal in his hand, which he had taken from the altar with tongs. He touched my mouth with it and said, "Behold, this has touched your lips; and your iniquity is taken away and your sin is forgiven."

Then I heard the voice of the Lord, saying, "Whom shall I send, and who will go for Us?" Then I said, "Here am I. Send me!"

Isaiah was ready for his calling . . . "Send me, Lord" . . . "Forgive me and send me out" . . . He was ready for whatever came his way . . . He was fired up to serve the Lord . . . He saw Jesus that day!

Simon Peter saw Jesus too . . . in a bit of a different way . . . but He saw Jesus and was able to *go* with Jesus.

Luke 5:1–11:

Now it happened that while the crowd was pressing around Him and listening to the word of God, He was standing by the lake of Gennesaret; and He saw two boats lying at the edge of the lake; but the fishermen had gotten out of them and were washing their nets. And He got into one of the boats, which was Simon's, and asked him to put out a little way from the land. And He sat down and began teaching the people from the boat. When He had finished speaking, He said to Simon, "Put out into the deep water and let down your nets for a catch." Simon answered and said, "Master, we worked hard all night and caught nothing, but I will do as You say and let down the nets." When they had done this, they enclosed a great quantity of fish, and their nets began to break; so they signaled to their partners in the other boat for them to come and help them. And they came and filled both of the boats, so that they began to sink. But when Simon Peter saw that, he fell down at Jesus' feet, saying, "Go away from me Lord, for I am a sinful man!" For amazement had seized him and all his companions because of the catch of fish which they had taken; and so also were James and John, sons of Zebedee, who were partners with Simon. And Jesus said to Simon, "Do not fear, from now on you will be catching men." When they had brought their boats to land, they left everything and followed Him.

Different kind of calling . . . one definitely more "regal" than the other . . . but a calling nonetheless . . . and a calling that Peter responded to. He knew he was sinful and needed Jesus. They gave up everything they had to follow Him.

God is calling you though His Word. It's right there in black and white . . . Sure, some is gray and up to interpretation that requires study . . . but don't fear that study . . . let it fire you up. When we were children we memorized God's Word . . . we "hid" it in our hearts. That is still important today . . . Take a small chunk of Scripture and hide it your heart. It will bless you! Share with others that Word. The Word is as alive today as it was when God inspired those authors to write it.

2 Timothy 2:15: "Be diligent to present yourself approved to God as a workman who does not need to be ashamed, accurately handling the word of truth."

There's a small nugget to memorize for you . . . "Preach the Gospel . . . use words if necessary" (St. Francis of Assisi).

Have a great Thursday! Remember this Christmas He chose you!

Friday

I love emojis <insert emoticon>

I hope this post finds you in the midst of a great morning and not seeing the calendar date that is very close to the big day. Let that go for now!

My heart has a lot going on right now and I want to share something that you can take with you and share with others today.

Prayer has become so important in our lives here at The Hadden's. We really try to make it our first thing instead of our last thing . . . something kept in our back pocket for a rainy day. God wants to hear from you right away. Giving things to Him right away really shows Him you love and trust Him. The devil has another plan . . . to accuse you . . . that is his job . . . it's in his name. The devil's job is to accuse you of all the sins that you do.

Revelations 12:10–12:

Then I heard a loud voice in heaven, saying, "Now the salvation, and the power, and the kingdom of our God and the authority of His Christ have come, for the accuser of our brethren has been thrown down, he who accuses them before our God day and night. And they overcame him because of the blood of the Lamb and

70

because of the word of their testimony, and they did not love their life even when faced with death. For this reason, rejoice, O heavens and you who dwell in them. Woe to the earth and the sea, because the devil has come down to you, having great wrath, knowing that he has only a short time.

The devil has only a short time and he is working now! But . . . don't be afraid . . . prayer is our power . . . praying Scripture is our power! The devil wants to shut your mouth . . . so open that mouth and scare that enemy away. Your tongue is spiritual fire. Release that POWER! Jesus forgave your sin and you have been made clean . . . let someone know! Don't let the Accuser have today. Take it!

Psalm 124:3–8:

Then they would have swallowed us alive, when their anger was kindled against us; Then the waters would have engulfed us, the stream would have swept over our soul; Then the raging waters would have swept over our soul. Blessed be the LORD, who has not given us to be torn by their teeth. Our soul has escaped as a bird out of the snare of the trapper; The snare is broken, and we have escaped. Our help is in the name of the LORD, who made heaven and earth.

Your snare is broken today! How amazing is that. See that huge amazing gift Jesus gave you by dying on that old wooden cross and rising again for you! He knew you by name. With His blood He said I died for _____ (put your name there!).

Have a wonderful Friday! Go tell it on the mountain that Jesus Christ is born for you! He chose YOU! 🙂

Saturday

*G*ood morning, friends

Getting up this morning at nine was such a huge treat. I hope you all were able to get some extra rest before your Christmas activities.

Today, I was reading John 13:1–20:

"Now before the Feast of the Passover, Jesus knowing that His hour had come that He would depart out of this world to the Father, having loved His own who were in the world, He loved them to the end. During supper, the devil having already put into the heart of Judas Iscariot, the son of Simon, to betray Him, Jesus, knowing that the Father had given all things into His hands, and that He had come forth from God and was going back to God, got up from supper, and laid aside His garments; and taking a towel, He girded Himself. Then He poured water into the basin, and began to wash the disciples' feet and to wipe them with the towel with which He was girded. So He came to Simon Peter. He said to Him, "Lord, do You wash my feet?" Jesus answered and said to him, "What I do you do not real-ize now, but you will understand hereaf-ter." Peter said to Him, "Never shall You wash my feet!" Jesus answered him, "If I do not wash you, you have no part with Me." Simon Peter said to Him, "Lord, then wash not only my feet, but also my hands and my head." Jesus said to him, "He who has bathed needs only to wash his feet, but is completely clean; and you are clean, but not all of you." For He knew the one who was betraying Him; for this reason He said, "Not all of you are clean." So when He had washed their feet, and taken His garments and reclined at the table again, He said to them, "Do you know what I have done to you? You call Me Teacher and Lord; and you are right, for so I am. If I then, the Lord and the Teacher, washed your feet, you also ought to wash one another's feet. For I gave you an example that you also should do as I did to you. Truly, truly, I say to you, a slave is not greater than his master, nor is one who is sent greater than the one who sent him. If you know these things, you are blessed if you do them. I do not speak of all of you. I know the ones I have cho-sen; but it is that the Scripture may be ful-filled, 'HE WHO EATS MY BREAD HAS LIFTED UP HIS HEEL AGAINST ME.' From now on I am telling you before it comes to pass, so that when it does occur, you may believe that I am He. Truly, truly, I say to you, he who receives whomever I send receives Me; and he who receives Me receives Him who sent Me."

Washing feet . . . yuck! The host had the pleasure to wash those dirty feet. We have seen do many things that you wouldn't expect the King of Heaven to do . . . but Jesus is showing how to be a true servant . . . and being a true servant is to make yourself truly unselfish and put yourself out there and do things you wouldn't normally do.

Being a true servant? How can we do that? Put others before ourselves. Jesus did it on the cross. We can do just the same . . . prayer is a great start. Who can you pray for today? Who can you reach out to and just give them some encouragement?

Loving those who seem unlovable is something that I have been trying to practice . . . knowing that sometimes you can't fix the situation, but you can just love where they are . . . even they do things that you wouldn't, but you love them through it . . . that is the hardest. You can't fix everything, but you know how to just love them where they are.

Have a wonderful Christmas Eve Eve!

Remember He chose you! 🐾

Date: Sun, Dec 24, 2017 8:08 a.m.

Sunday

*H*appy Christmas Eve, my friends.

This is going to be a quick post because I have to get ready for church, which was my goal! I'm so excited to see God working in not only my life but so many of you going through this journey with us as well!

I wanted to just talk quickly about HOPE . . .

Romans 15:4: "For whatever was written in earlier times was written for our instruction, so that through perseverance and the encouragement of the Scriptures we might have hope."

We might have HOPE!

Hope means confidence, eager anticipation, expectation, longing, aspiration.

God showed up in a stable . . . He is showing up today . . . for you! Don't miss that hope! God is getting me to church . . . Where is He is sending you today?

Merry Christmas!

Love you all! 🦊

*M*erry Christmas!

I pray that all your little ones aren't up yet! The advantage of having teenagers is that they sleep through pretty much everything.

I woke up early this morning not so happy. I am being honest . . . it's hard to be a burden to your family day after day. My husband is truly the picture of Jesus Christ, because even though he willingly takes on the challenge of being my caretaker . . . it does get hard . . . and seeing that day in day out is difficult for me. I know that the devil wants me to give up and just wallow in sadness . . . but I'm not! I'm going to encourage you with something from Jesus!

Here's some of the lyrics from a Nichole Nordeman song . . . Just give them a read, and hopefully they are encouraging to you . . . Jesus loves us so much.

"Love You More"
Nichole Nordeman

You said, "Go and sin no more . . ."
Though my eyes could not meet Yours
I started running the third time the rooster
crowed
You threw a party just for me
Though I squandered everything
I was blinded in the middle of the road
Climbed up in a tree to see You
Swallowed by the sea to flee You

Sold You for a little silver and a kiss
Killed a man to love his woman
Burned a bridge back to Your garden
Hung beside You while you took Your
final breath
You've been loving me since time began
You're behind my every second chance
I love You
I'm trying to
Love You more
I'm ready
Please help me
Love You more
I keep thinking there's a limit
Sure, I must be getting near it
When I've used up every pardon and regret
But You promise there is freedom
Gathered up the broken pieces
Scattered them as far as East is from the
West
You've been loving me since time began
You're behind my every second chance
l love You
I'm trying to
Love You more
I'm ready
Please help me
Love You more
With all the sand that fills the hourglass
With every breath between my first and
last

I love You
I'm trying to
Love You more
I'm ready
Please help me
Love You more

Jesus loves us more . . . can't be described or paid back. Just wallow in it today. He is in the business of restoration and redemption, and I always seem to be talking about it . . . but it happened in my life and will continue, I am sure.

I'll tell you a story and then I will be letting you get to your Christmas.

I was sitting in my living room in horrible pain in October . . . maybe the second or third week, I don't really remember . . . but I know that I was praying for relief from the pain. I would cry on the couch for hours waiting for my Nathan to come home from school, so he could rub my foot, because that was literally the only thing that would give me relief for a few minutes. He always did it willingly. On this day I picked up my phone and just started texting my sister-in-law Lisa whom I talked to here and there but nothing consistent because, spoiler alert, I was a jerk! I started telling her how I was in the darkest place and God wasn't listening to me and how I was done. She texted some beautiful words of life from God's Word and then told me she wanted to come up on the weekend, and I just said yes immediately. That was the beginning of the restoration and redemption of my family. We were restored . . . and if that was all that would come out of this . . . then it is well worth it . . . but I know there's more . . . Encourage your walk with Jesus. The story continues. I don't know what I would do without my blood family but also my "other" family. God is so good . . . all the time.

Have the best Christmas today. Jesus chose to come for you. Don't miss that! Praying for you today.

Merry Christmas! 😊

I pray that Christmas was a great day of time with your family and friends and that you were able to watch the Eagles game without any heart attack.

We woke up a bit late this morning, and sometimes I just sit and wait to see what God has for me . . . I sat much longer than usual because it didn't come to me right away. I went through my journals and other resources that I use daily. I am doing a Gideon study with Pricilla Shirer, who is a gifted women's Bible teacher . . . very grounded in God's Word.

There are historical things when reading Judges that I would have flown over without going through this study . . . one of them is called the "Deliverance Principle" . . . A powerful kingdom would come in (called the suzerain) and would adopt the smaller kingdom (called the vassal). The larger kingdom would offer protection and give them what they needed. The larger kingdom had authority over the smaller kingdom. The smaller kingdom was to be loyal and keep the covenant with the larger nation. The Bible uses the Hebrew word *hesed* which means "love and faithful-ness." If you were in rebellion, you hated the larger country that adopted you.

Yahweh had a covenant like this with Abraham. Yahweh adopted Israel and commanded them to love Him with their heart, soul, mind, and strength (Deut. 6:5). This was the covenant . . . the deliverance principle . . .

Did the Israelites obey? Did they love and remain faithful? No! If you begin in Judges 2, Joshua dies, and they begin to do whatever they please . . . they worship other gods . . . they live with those who they aren't supposed to . . . but God loves them always and gives them judges to save them . . . but once that judge dies . . . they go back to the horrible way they had acted.

This is all part of God's beautiful redemption story . . . the main message of God's Word is God's redemption of humanity. No matter what you do . . . the God of the heavens wants you back! God loves you today and every day and wants you to be His. Going to Him in prayer first . . . be with Him first . . . be part of that redemption story.

And . . . there was a remnant speaking truth to the Israelites during that time . . . There's a remnant boldly speaking truth during our time . . . Be that remnant . . . Get into the Word and soak up God's truth and share it with those around you.

Have a wonderful Tuesday!

I hope this last week of 2017 is full of fun for you and your family. We attempted to go see *Star Wars* yesterday . . . which didn't work out because the lines were long and confusing so we decided to go to eat and see it another time. It was a day out, so I am always appreciative of that!

Nine words for you today . . . "Yet not my will but what you will, God!" This is how we need to pray . . . It is the hardest way to pray, but it is putting God in the driver's seat . . . and knowing that He is Good!

Jesus prayed this in the Garden of Gethsemane . . . surrounded by the trees that He created. I was watching a talk by Lysa Terkeust this morning . . . She had three facts about the olive . . .

1. The olive tree cannot produce unless there are hot winds from the desert and there are refreshing winds from the Mediterranean. (Good times and bad times will produce fruit.)
2. When it produces fruit . . . you can't eat that fruit right away . . . it needs to be prepared and proven.
3. The oil is the most used part of the olive and it is pressed three times:

First press: healing oil
Second press: food prep
Third press: light

Jesus knew the message of the olive . . . As He sat there and waited His "fate" that He chose but I think dealing with the emotions of what was going to happen finally was sinking in. His Father God was going to turn His back on Jesus, and that was maybe crashing down on Jesus.

The story of redemption is written in the Bible between two Gardens . . . Eden, which was messed up with sin and we would never be able to be there . . . and there is one at the end of Revelations . . . a perfect place that we will live in forever . . . a perfect place that we will inhabit and worship our God. To be include in this garden . . . all you have to do is say YES to Jesus . . . He loves you and died for you.

Your circumstances may not be good . . . But God Is Good! Remember that today. Tell someone that today.

Have a wonderful Wednesday!

I am trying to formulate my thoughts to give something that can encourage you today. Last night I was fighting a horrible chest cold and the cough was painful . . . but this morning I feel so much better. My dearest hubby got me a Chromebook, so I am able to use a "real" keyboard to post! Please feel free to repost anything that you think would help others.

It's quiet here this morning. Bob has some errands to run and he took the boys, and Emmie is out with friends . . . so I am able to put some praise music on to focus on the Lord!

WORSHIP! There's a king named Jehoshaphat who relied on worship to win a battle. He got word from his "CIA" that many forces were coming to destroy Israel. This was Jehoshaphat's response . . .

Chronicles 20:3–4: "Alarmed, Jehoshaphat resolved to inquire of the Lord, and he proclaimed a fast for all Judah. The people of Judah came together to seek help from the Lord; indeed, they came from every town in Judah to seek him."

His first response was prayer and fasting! And then we get to the battle . . .

2 Chronicles 20:15–17: He said: "Listen, King Jehoshaphat and all who live in Judah and Jerusalem! This is what the Lord says to you: 'Do not be afraid or discouraged because of this vast army. For the battle is not yours, but God's. Tomorrow march down against them. They will be climbing up by the Pass of Ziz, and you will find them

at the end of the gorge in the Desert of Jeruel. You will not have to fight this battle. Take up your positions; stand firm and see the deliverance the Lord will give you, Judah and Jerusalem. Do not be afraid; do not be discouraged. Go out to face them tomorrow, and the Lord will be with you.'"

So Jehoshaphat goes to face them early in the morning with a praise and worship band . . .

2 Chronicles 20:21 (The Message): After talking it over with the people, Jehoshaphat appointed a choir for God, dressed in holy robes, they were to march head of the troops, singing "Give thanks to God, His love never quits."

2 Chronicles 20:22–23 (The Message): "As soon as they started shouting and praising, God set ambushes against the men of Ammon, Moab and Mount Seir and massacred them. Then further confused, they went at each other and all ended up killed."

Now, the end of Jehoshaphat's life wasn't as successful as this battle because he decided to do business with other kingdoms instead of getting rid of them as God told all the kings of Israel to do.

Prayer, praise, and worship . . . what a way to start your day . . . start your search for answers . . . start anything. God wants to hear from you right away . . . and hear your love for Him. He also wants to hear that you have absolute trust in Him even when things look the worst.

Have a great Thursday!

Good morning . . . is it still morning? Today is the day that the Lord has made, and I am out of it.:) Ha! My children have an amazing gift of sleeping until noon and thereafter.

This morning I was reading from Romans 1:1–17 where Paul wants to get to Rome in the worst way, but every time he can't get there for many reasons.

Romans 1:16: "For I am not ashamed of the gospel, because it is the power of God that brings SALVATION to everyone who believes, first to the Jew and then to the Gentile."

Paul shows in Romans the true biblical account of God's rescue of all of us . . . the rescue that includes Jesus's life, death, and resurrection. Paul shows that he is not ashamed of this message and will boldly go anywhere he needs to go to share the news of Jesus. Paul also shows that he is a sinner and is weak and needs Jesus just as much as those he is talking to.

It's important that all people understand that it's not just a story . . . but it's the real-life rescue of all people by the powerful HAND OF GOD!

Have a great Friday. Don't waste a second.

Good morning, my friends! Maybe you are able to relax and enjoy the snow this morning . . . and hopefully out the window! I am listening to some praise music by Michael W. Smith and reading the book of Romans. Romans is a difficult book but has truth put there directly by Jesus Christ.

The passage I have been reading this morning is Romans 1:18–32, "God's Wrath Against Sinful Humanity":

> The wrath of God is being revealed from heaven against all the godlessness and wickedness of people, who suppress the truth by their wickedness, since what may be known about God is plain to them, because God has made it plain to them. For since the creation of the world God's invisible qualities—his eternal power and divine nature—have been clearly seen, being understood from what has been made. So that people are without excuse for although they knew God, they neither glorified him as God nor gave thanks to him, but their thinking became futile and their foolish hearts were darkened. Although they claimed to be wise, they became foolishness and exchanged the glory of the immortal God for images made to look like a mortal human being

and birds and animals and reptiles. Therefore God gave them over in the sinful desires of their hearts to sexual impurity for the degrading of their bodies with one another. They exchanged the truth about God for a lie, and worshiped and served created things rather than the Creator— who is forever praised. Amen. Because of this, God gave them over to shameful lusts. Even their women exchanged natural sexual relations for unnatural ones. In the same way the men also abandoned natural relations with women and were inflamed with lust for one another. Men committed shameful acts with other men and received in themselves the due penalty for their error. Furthermore, just as they did not think it worthwhile to retain the knowledge of God, so God gave them over to a depraved mind, so that they do what ought not to be done. They have become filled with every kind of wickedness, evil, greed, and depravity. They are full of envy, murder, strife, deceit, and malice. They are gossips, slanderers, God-haters, insolent, arrogant and boastful; they invent ways of doing evil; they disobey their parents; they have no understanding, no fidelity, no love, no mercy. Although they know God's righteous decree that those who do such things deserve death, they not only continue to do these very things but also approve of those who practice them.

This passage is so difficult because so many have different translations to make it more "tolerable" for those we love . . . and a loving God would never say these things (like "deserve death"). These end times are upon us and things get worse every day, I believe that is why we are so drawn to the Hallmark Channel because those movies guarantee a happy ending in two hours . . . and it's a clean happy. Turning on the news cannot guarantee a clean and happy ending . . . it is violence and what is described in this passage.

We have to speak truth about these times, without fear. God opposes sin because God is Good, righteous, and JUST. We cannot speak the Good NEWS of God's SALVATION without talking about the bad . . . we are sinners. We can't call it SALVATION if we aren't saying that we are being SAVED from something BAD . . . our sin!

This is TRUTH. It's not my truth . . . it's in the Bible . . . it's black and white, and avoiding it isn't love . . . it's just avoiding what is there and what will hurt you in eternity.

Proverbs 1:7: "The fear of the Lord is the beginning of knowledge, fools despise wisdom and instruction."

2 Timothy 3:1–5: "But understand this, that yin the last days there will come times of difficulty. For people will be lovers of self, lovers of money, proud, arrogant, abusive, disobedient to their parents, ungrateful, unholy, heartless, unappeasable, slanderous, without self-control, brutal, not loving good, treacherous, reckless, swollen with conceit, lovers of pleasure rather than lovers of God, having the

appearance of godliness, but denying its power. Avoid such people."

Call on Jesus . . . Jesus loves you . . .

"Jesus"
by Chris Tomlin

There is a truth older than the ages
There is a promise of things yet to come
There is one, born for our salvation
Jesus
There is a light that overwhelms the darkness
There is a kingdom that forever reigns
There is freedom from the chains that bind us
Jesus, Jesus
Who walks on the waters
Who speaks to the sea
Who stands in the fire beside me
He roars like a lion
He bled as the iamb
He carries my healing in his hands
Jesus
There is a name I call in times of trouble
There is a song that comforts in the night
There is a voice that calms the storm that rages
He is Jesus, Jesus
Who walks on the waters
Who speaks to the sea

Who stands in the fire beside me
He roars like a lion
He bled as the lamb
He carries my healing in his hands

Have a great and snowy day. 😊

Date: Tue, Jan 2, 2018 10:12 a.m.

*H*appy New Year's to you and your family. Our family has been fighting upper respiratory problems over here since before New Year's Eve. It has been miserable. God has been faithful and allowed us to have a rest and a time where we don't have "schedules" to follow or anywhere we had to be.

It has been pretty "dark," though. The darkness I talk about is just the feeling "What is this teaching me?" . . . "Why are we going through this?" . . . and the classic "Why me, Lord?" These are joy stealers for sure. Hope stealers. I am here to be encouraging . . . but I don't feel encouraging . . . we put a lot of stock in our feelings, but we can't be ruled by them.

Here enters God's Word! God's Word is so important . . . We need it for everyday life and when we abandon that . . . things get worse.

John 10:1–6 (ESV):

I Am the Good Shepherd

"Truly, truly, I say to you, he who does not enter the sheepfold by the door but climbs in by another way, that man is a thief and a robber. But he who enters by the door is the shepherd of the sheep. To him the gatekeeper opens. The sheep hear his voice, and he calls his own sheep by name and leads them out. When he has brought out all his own, he goes before them, and the sheep follow him, for they know his voice. A stranger they will not follow, but they will flee from him, for they do not know the voice of strangers." This figure of speech Jesus used with them, but they did not understand what he was saying to them.

Jesus is the Good Shepherd calling to us . . . calling us to Him . . .

The shepherd referenced in Jesus's time devoted all his time to his sheep . . . they knew his voice even with thousands of sheep around him . . . thousands! Do you know your shepherd . . . with thousands of voices around you . . . do you know your Shepherd?

In the darkness, I hear voices that aren't of God . . . they are demonic I am sure . . . trying to grab that encouragement/hope/joy/peace . . . you name it . . . they are trying to take it from me. Prayer is the weapon . . . spiritual discernment is what I need . . . what we all need.

What can you do today? Back to work/school/generally same activities that you were delighted not to do for a few days . . . Can you offer a smile/hug/prayer/love to those who are really hard, hard, hard to love?

I got a voicemail message from someone during Christmas vacation . . . and she is sooo hard to love . . . so hard . . . And she said, "Susan . . . I just wanted you to know I love you . . . I really, really love you." It was just so wonderful . . . broke my heart that I dismissed her for so long . . . but I know that she loves me so much . . . it was just amazing.

God is so into the business of miracles and answered prayer . . . and making His Word ALIVE.

Have a wonderful Tuesday!

Date: Wed, Jan 3, 2018 7:49 a.m.

*H*appy Wonderful Wednesday . . . the sun is shining, and we have some hopes of snow.

This morning the Lord has definitely been speaking to me, and I want to share every tidbit I can to encourage you. The Lord brings me back to the passage in Genesis 2 and 3 about Adam and Eve and the choice they made in the garden of Eden. The message that they heard was SHAME!

The very first words we hear from Satan is questioning the authority of Scripture . . . "You won't be like that" . . . "Who told you that?" . . . You will believe the lies you hear from the devil if you don't know your Bible . . . He'll say, "That isn't what it means" . . . "Well, if you interpret it like this, it doesn't mean that," etc., etc., etc. NOT TODAY, DEVIL!

The devil gives us FEAR/SHAME/HIDING . . . but that isn't where we need to be looking . . . YOU ARE THE DAUGHTER/SON OF THE KING . . . YOU WEREN'T built for SHAME. THERE IS NO CONDEMNATION!

Christianity is not behavior modification for our world . . . Many "Christians" say . . . your Bible is:

Not tolerant enough (say this to your boyfriend/girlfriend/wife/husband: "I tolerate you." Sounds pretty, right?).

Too legalistic.
Not inclusive.
Too judgmental.
IF WE BELIEVE THESE THINGS WE DON'T KNOW THE GOSPEL!

Romans 1:16–17 (ESV):

The Righteous Shall Live by Faith

For I am not ashamed of the gospel, for it is the power of God for salvation to everyone who believes, to the Jew first and also to the Greek. For in it the righteousness of God is revealed from faith for faith, as it is written, "The righteous shall live by faith."

You were not built for shame!

Acts 4:13–22:

Now when they saw the boldness of Peter and John, and perceived that they were Now when they saw the boldness of Peter and John, and perceived that they were uneducated, common men, they were astonished. And they recognized that they had been with Jesus. But seeing the man who was healed standing beside them, they had nothing to say in opposition. But when they had commanded them to leave the council, they conferred with one another, saying, "What shall we do with these men? For that is notable sign has been performed through them is evident to all the inhabitants of Jerusalem, and we cannot deny it. But in order that it may spread no further among the people, let us warn them to speak no more to anyone in this name." So they called them and charged them not to speak or teach at all in the name of Jesus. But Peter and John answered them, k "Whether it is right in the sight of God to listen to you rather than to God, you must judge, for I cannot but speak of what we have seen and heard." And when they had further threatened them, they let them go, finding no way to punish them, because of the people, for all were praising God for what had happened. For the man on whom this sign of healing was performed was more than forty years old. uneducated, common men, they were astonished. And they recognized that they had been with Jesus.

Jesus is Alive and setting people free . . . and our schools (colleges/high schools/middle schools/elementary schools) need students/teachers/staff/parents/alumni to speak up . . . be the remnant that says . . . "Who told you that you were naked, dumb, unlovable, ugly . . . etc.?"

You shall know the truth and the truth will set you free . . .

You are set free!

You are set free . . . TODAY!

*H*appy Snow Day . . . it is really coming down . . . and if you were those people who told me it was going to be nothing . . . well . . . God answers prayers! There's your proof!

I was able to sleep a bit later and feel better but still have this lingering cough that is just annoying. Please continue to pray that it goes away.

I have been watching some sermons from the Passion Conference which is from Louie Giglio's church. It is for high school, college, and career . . . you know, the young-sters, but it is chock full of stuff that we "older" people can use as well.

This social media society that we are living in is totally in effect in every age group. I encourage people to "follow me" or "friend me" on Facebook/Instagram, etc. . . . but it is definitely not to impress anyone . . . or to have the most "followers" of all time.

God doesn't care about your popularity or your follow-ers on any social media! He cares about your walk . . . walk with integrity.

Satan knows a few things about you.

You have been forgiven.

There is no condemnation.

You have been given the victory.

There is no shame.

There is no guilt.

Satan knows the END . . . he is FINISHED!

HE wants you to be discouraged with fear.

He has EVIL schemes and he is watching you . . . trying to trip you up . . . so you need the WHOLE ARMOR OF GOD!

Ephesians 6:10–21 (NIV):

> The Armor of God: Finally, be strong in the Lord and in his mighty power. Put on the full armor of God, so that you can take your stand against the devil's schemes. For our struggle is not against flesh and blood, but against the rulers, against the authorities, against the powers of this dark world and against the spiritual forces of evil in the heavenly realms. Therefore, put on the full armor of God, so that when the day of evil comes, you may be able to stand your ground, and after you have done everything, to stand. Stand firm then, with the belt of truth buckled around your waist, with the breastplate of righteousness in place, and with your feet fitted with the readiness that comes from the gospel of peace. In addition to all this, take up the shield of faith, with which you can extinguish all the flaming arrows of the evil one. Take the helmet of salvation and the sword of the Spirit, which is the word of God. And pray in the Spirit on all occasions with all kinds of prayers and requests. With this in mind, be alert and always keep on praying for all the Lord's

people. Pray also for me, that whenever I speak, words may be given me so that I will fearlessly make known the mystery of the gospel, for which I am an ambassador in chains. Pray that I may declare it fearlessly, as I should.

The Armor of God:

Breastplate of Righteousness
Belt of Truth
Gospel of Peace
Helmet of Salvation
Sword of the Spirit (Word of God)
PRAYER!

Prayer is the key that unlocks the resources of heaven so that they can be unleashed on planet EARTH! Prayer is what pushes the kingdom of darkness back!

HOLINESS is your breastplate! BE YE HOLY. Holiness is what holds the kingdom of darkness back . . . like my Bible professor used to say . . . "If the plain sense makes good sense, seek no other sense." Don't water down God's Word. We don't concentrate on holiness anymore . . . we concentrate on not offending people so they stay, they stay our friends . . . and in our churches.

Our churches need to be houses of prayer, not houses of cool worship teams/coffee houses/flashy lights, etc. Don't get me wrong, these things are nice and enjoyable, and many times enhance our church experience, but if that is what you are going for . . . a pre-seeker church, where if you offend them with the Gospel of Jesus because you speak the truth about sin and their need for a Savior they will BOLT. God specifically in black and white says that His house will be a house of prayer . . . and truth . . . and love . . . and grace . . . and mercy . . . etc.

In short . . . let's get back to Holiness . . . and God's grace, mercy, love, integrity, and TRUTH! Don't be afraid of offense. Jesus met the woman at the well . . . knew her sin . . . told her . . . and told her, "GO AND SIN NO MORE." He didn't say, "Thanks for the drink, you're cool." He never let anyone go away in their sin! He wanted them to be forgiven and not do that anymore. Of course, perfection is impossible, but you will want to love and serve God because He chose to save you . . . He died for you . . . and that LOVE compels you to want to love and obey HIM.

Galatians 5:1 (NIV): "Freedom in Christ: It is for freedom that Christ has set us free. Stand firm, then, and do not let yourselves be burdened again by a yoke of slavery."

Delivered in November 2018
by Elder William Rodebaugh at Olivet Covenant Presbyterian Church

Why?

$\mathcal{A}$ number of years ago, I became aware of a book, actually two books, by Josh McDowell, *Questions That Deserve an Answer*, one and two.

Now, I never read the books, only heard about them and a synopsis. There was another book by I believe the same author, *Why Bad Things Happen to Good People*.

Now, as you well know, I'm not a theologian or anyone who is fully conversant of all that Scripture has to say on this subject. I'm just someone who believes.

So, when I see things that happen in the world—and I'm not impacted by these events, I say, as I believe it is God's will. There are murders. Fifty-eight in Las Vegas and twenty-six in Texas. There were storms in Texas, Florida, Puerto Rico. Hurricane Maria impacted members of Olivet. Andy and Daisy and a good friend of ours had their homes damaged and suffered injury. Daisy and Andy can ask, why? Not questioning "Why, God, to me and not someone else?" But: "Why did it happen, and where do we go from here?"

Romans 8:28 tells us that "all things work together for good to those who love God." Do we really believe this in our hearts? A great verse to fall back on if you believe. In John's Gospel the disciples asked the reason for the young man's blindness. Who sinned? Christ gave the answer: It was for a purpose and not a penalty for sin. So, we not know or understand why immediately. We may not see anything good coming out of a disaster, injury, sickness, or death when it first strikes home.

I'd like to continue not giving a typical sermon, but more like telling you a story. A story that to me is amazing. A story that exhibits the power of prayer, God's timing, and God's family. How did it come about? What started it? Where do we go from here?

The story begins about a decade ago when a grumpy old man raised his voice at a grandson because the grandson did something he was told not to do. His carelessness broke something worth about ten dollars, including shipping and handling.

The grandson's mother chastised Mr. Grumpy, who realized he shouldn't have raised his voice to the grandchild.

What Mr. Grumpy did was the final straw in a long line of misunderstandings. All parents know the misunderstanding that "Daddy loves you more than he loves me." In this case it's about grandchildren.

A decade of daily prayer didn't bring reconciliation. Postcards from travels. Christmas cards, emails, and cold receptions from family events went for naught. Mr. Grumpy did even dumber stuff over the years.

Then in God's own time a daughter-in-law writes on Facebook a memory about two miscarriages. So, Mr. Grumpy, who is older and wiser but not smarter, responds to the post. He mentions that something similar had happened, and after that a wonderful daughter was born. The pride of his life. The same thing happened in the life of the daughter-in-law. A beautiful daughter was born.

Grumpy must have touched a nerve, as after a decade of silence the daughter made contact through her brother. She asks her brother how she should contact the parents. The brother took it upon himself to talk with the parents, and the next day contact was made. There was a phone call and crying and talk.

Wouldn't it be wonderful if the family came together? A great family reunion. Hugs and kisses, love abounding, and all things forgiven. But it didn't work out that way. Remember Romans 8:28!

But let me tell you about the daughter. She is beautiful. Has a giving heart. Has a lovely voice. Is a fine schoolteacher. A mother of four, ages sixteen to ten. Things I remember, like the love she showed her grandmother by taking her hand when we visited the nursing home even though the grandmother didn't know who we were. The time she stood up for someone wrongly accused in high school, even though she wasn't friends with the girl. We hear she stood up for Christ at the risk of losing her job. Now she wasn't perfect. By accident she set fire to her mattress and twice left lipstick in her pocket in the wash, which made a mess. I'm sure there are many more positives I can relate. Very few negatives.

Now it's time to meet face to face. The meeting was tearful when realizing that there was an injury resulting in hip damage and severe pain. But as we were to find out that the injured hip was the ultimate reason for the pain.

The reason for the pain is a very rare cancer. This was discovered from a parent's realization that a good friend had a contact with a surgeon. The daughter had been waiting to hear from a doctor of this caliber for a long time. Through the friend the doctor made immediate contact and set up an appointment. That doctor didn't think the pain was a result of the hip injury and discussed the problem with a neurologist and eventually the final diagnosis.

So let's recap the events: Misunderstanding happened a decade ago. No meaningful contact. Prayers are made daily. God used Facebook—and I hate social media—to bring the family together. Injury is discovered to be more serious, and God through a friend gets things going.

God has also provided literally hundreds of people praying for a cure. A member of Olivet has put the family in touch with people who may be able to help.

The story continues, and the final answer is in the future. God knows the answer and the outcome. We pray that His will and ours is the same.

But it doesn't answer the question, "Why?" We don't know the future. We wish for the best, but as we read in Romans, God knows the best.

We ask why, but we sometimes forget what happened two thousand years ago.

As Christians we believe in Christ. One of my favorite statements is Peter's confession, "You are the Christ. The Son of the Living God." We believe as it is said in John

3:16, "For God so loved the world He gave His only begotten son."

We can't forget that God let His only Son be tortured and unjustly murdered for us. God turned His back on His son on the cross because God couldn't look upon the sins of the world that Christ took upon himself. God could have called ten thousand angels, as the son goes, to save Christ, but let His son die for you and me.

So, the question of why still stands. The answer: we don't know. But what we do know is that God is in control, and whatever the outcome, we know God only wants the best for those who love Him.

About the Author

Bill is the loving husband of fifty-one years to Eydie Rodebaugh and father of Bill Junior and Susan Rodebaugh Hadden. He has nine grandchildren, two granddaughters and seven grandsons. Bill, a retired commercial underwriting manager, is a Ruling Elder and deacon of Olivet Covenant Presbyterian Church in Philadelphia, Pennsylvania. For twenty years, Bill was the president and secretary of the Board of the Helping Hand Rescue Mission in Philadelphia. Bill has published *Dad: It Takes a Dad*. The Rodebaughs are active in Christian education, working with and supporting the Children's Jubilee Fund, which provides scholarship for needy children applying to Christian Schools.